Ancient Civilizations

Published by Creative Paperbacks
P.O. Box 227, Mankato, Minnesota 56002
Creative Paperbacks is an imprint of
THE CREATIVE COMPANY
www.thecreativecompany.us

Design and production by CHRISTINE VANDERBEEK
Art direction by RITA MARSHALL

Printed in the United States of America

PHOTOGRAPHS BY Alamy (Henry Westheim
Photography, North Wind Picture Archives), Corbis
(Jerry Arcieri, Burstein Collection, Yi Lu/Viewstock,
Royal Ontario Museum, Keren Su), Getty Images
(Izabela Habur), SuperStock (The Art Archive;
Blue Jean Images; Bridgeman Art Library, London;
DeAgostini; Exactostock; David Forbert; Fotosearch;
Stock Connection; SuperStock), Wikipedia (vlasta2)

LIBRARY OF CONGRESS
CATALOGING-IN-PUBLICATION DATA
Bodden, Valerie.
China / by Valerie Bodden.
p. cm. — (Ancient civilizations)
Includes bibliographical references and index.
SUMMARY: A historical overview of dynastic China from
the perspectives of the social classes, from the royals to
the peasants, including the Chinese empire's growth and
decline.

ISBN 978-1-60818-391-3 (HARDCOVER)
ISBN 978-0-89812-978-6 (PBK)
1. China—Civilization. I. Title.

DS721.B6134 2014
951—dc23   2013032511

CCSS: RI.5.1, 2, 3, 5, 6, 8, 9; RH.6-8.4, 5, 6, 7, 8, 9

FIRST EDITION
9 8 7 6 5 4 3 2 1

CHINA

VALERIE BODDEN

TABLE OF CONTENTS

INTRODUCTION

China is among the oldest existing civilizations in the world. ***Nomadic*** peoples wandered through much of what is now China more than 12,000 years ago. By around 7000 B.C., many of those peoples had begun to settle along China's rivers, including the Yellow River in the north and the Yangtze in the south. There they began to farm and raise animals.

Over time, farming settlements joined together to form states. Eventually, some states became stronger than others. They conquered their neighbors and established ***dynasties*** that ruled over China. The early history of China can be divided into five main dynasties: the Xia (*SHAH*) ruled from about 2070 to 1600 B.C.; the Shang from around 1600 to 1046 B.C.; the Zhou

The longest river in Asia, the Yangtze has influenced Chinese history from its beginning.

(*JO*) from 1046 to 221 B.C.; the Qin (*CHIN*) from 221 to 206 B.C.; and the Han from 206 B.C. to A.D. 220.

The land that constituted "China" varied from dynasty to dynasty, reaching its farthest extent under the Han. The Chinese considered their land to be the center of the world and called it Zhongguo, or the "Middle Kingdom." Anyone outside China's borders was considered a barbarian. Natural barriers—including the Himalayas to the west; vast, empty plains to the north; and ocean to the south and east—kept China separate from outsiders. Although China was made up of many different cultural groups and eventually stretched more than 1,000 miles (1,610 km) from north to south and from east to west, its peoples were united by similar languages and cultures.

As China's dynasties changed, so did its so-

CHINA CIRCA A.D. 220

cial order. Under the Shang and early Zhou, China was set up as a *feudal* society. The king gave control over various states to members of the royal family. In return, the rulers of the states remained loyal to the king. There was little opportunity to climb the social ladder, since it was only by birth into the royal family that a person obtained a government position. By the end of the Zhou dynasty, however, social mobility had become a reality. Government officials now received their position on the basis of merit rather than birth. Peasant farmers who once worked for feudal lords had the opportunity to purchase their own land, and merchants often amassed riches equal to those of rulers. In some cases, members of the lower classes became educated and were able to reach the top offices in the country—including that of emperor.

Sections of the Great Wall still intact today are reminders of China's long dynastic history.

SONS OF HEAVEN

Scholars believe that China was first united under a king during the Xia dynasty, although they know little else about this time period. The first written Chinese records date from the Shang dynasty and reveal that the Shang king served largely as a priest. In a society that worshiped ancestors, the king received his authority because he was descended from the royal ancestors. He was believed to be able to communicate with them on behalf of the Chinese people.

The Shang kingship was hereditary. But it did not pass from father to son. Instead, it passed to the king's next oldest brother. After the throne had passed to all the king's brothers, it went to the oldest son of the oldest brother. In this way, the Shang throne was

The earliest bronze artifacts from China were made during the Shang dynasty.

passed down to 30 kings.

Then, in 1046, the Shang were defeated by an army from the state of Zhou, on the western edge of China. The Zhou justified their overthrow of the Shang king by saying that he was corrupt, so the god Tian (Heaven) no longer saw him as fit to rule. Instead, the Mandate of Heaven, or command to rule, had been given to the Zhou. From then on, all Chinese kings and emperors were believed to hold the Mandate of Heaven. If a king failed to rule well, he could be overthrown, and the mandate would be given to a new king.

Because he held the Mandate of Heaven, the Zhou king was considered the Son of Heaven. As the Son of Heaven, the king represented the will of the gods. Obeying him was the same as obeying Heaven. The Zhou kingship passed from father to son.

In 771 B.C., the Zhou capital Hao was defeated by barbarian warriors, and the Zhou were forced to move farther east, initiating a period known as the Eastern Zhou, which lasted until 221 B.C. The first part of the Eastern Zhou, from 770 to 476 B.C., is known as the Spring and Autumn period (named after a historical

Did You Know?

THE TOMB OF LADY HAO,

A MEMBER OF THE SHANG

ROYAL FAMILY, CONTAINED

16 HUMAN SACRIFICES,

130 BRONZE WEAPONS,

750 **JADE** OBJECTS, AND

70 STONE SCULPTURES.

work from the time). During this time, the king lost much of his centralized political authority. Rulers from the various states gained power, and many began to act independently from the king. During the second part of the Eastern Zhou, known as the Warring States period, seven states vied for power over all the states.

In 221 B.C., the state of Qin emerged victorious from the Warring States period, initiating the Qin dynasty—and the Chinese empire. The first Qin ruler took the title Shi Huangdi, or First Sovereign Emperor. Shi Huangdi was a harsh ruler, and when he died in 210 B.C., there was no strong successor to take his place. The Qin government was overthrown four years later.

In its place, the Han dynasty arose. Its first leader was Liu Bang, who had been born a peasant. Despite his humble background, Liu Bang came to be known as Gaozu, or "Great Ancestor," and he was worshiped by Han leaders long after his death. Under Gaozu and his successors, China nearly doubled in size, and ancient Chinese culture reached a high point.

Han emperors often had many wives. They usually chose one to be their primary wife, and

Shi Huangdi came from the state of Qin, a word from which historians think "China" originates.

Did You Know?

———

SCHOLARS BELIEVE

THAT AT LEAST 85 MASTER

CRAFTSMEN—ALONG

WITH THOUSANDS OF

ASSISTANTS—MADE THE

TERRACOTTA SOLDIERS

FOR SHI HUANGDI'S TOMB.

———

she was given the title empress. (The other wives were called concubines.) If her husband died, an empress became an empress dowager. If her son was too young to rule on his own, the empress dowager might rule alongside him.

The emperor, his empress and concubines, and their children lived in lavish wooden palaces. Most palaces were made up of several buildings connected by raised, roofed hallways. Bright murals covered the walls, and the roofs were made of decorated ceramic tiles. During the Han dynasty, palace grounds often included elaborate gardens and parks dotted with man-made lakes. The parks might be stocked with exotic animals—such as tigers, panthers, and bears—from across China. The emperor spent part of his leisure time hunting these animals.

The emperor lived at the center of his ***imperial*** complex. He was waited on by a large team of guards and servants. Because the emperor was the Son of Heaven, he had to follow a number of rituals in his daily life. He lived in different parts of the imperial palace at different times of the year. He also wore different colors and ate different foods based on the season. This was supposed to ensure that he—and thus all of China—remained in harmony with nature through the changing seasons.

Even as the emperors took part in the necessary rituals of their daily lives, they also prepared for the afterlife by building elaborate tombs. From the time of the Shang on, a ruler's tomb could be up to 300 feet (91 m) long and 60 feet (18 m) deep. The tomb was stocked with thousands of items, including cowry (brightly colored shellfish) shells, jade objects, and bronze vessels.

During the Shang period, kings were also buried with dozens or hundreds of victims of human sacrifice. Many victims were the king's relatives, women, nobles, guards, or servants. These people had served the king in life and were expected to continue to do so in death. Most probably volunteered for sacrifice. Some of the victims were slaves or prisoners of war, who were often beheaded before being buried. By the Zhou dynasty, human sacrifices were rarely carried out on such a large scale, possibly due to changes in religious beliefs.

During the Qin and Han dynasties, the tombs of emperors became even grander. The most stunning tomb was that of the first Qin emperor, Shi Huangdi. It was guarded by four pits filled with more than 8,000 life-sized terracotta, or clay, statues of soldiers and horses as well as wooden chariots. According to historical records, the burial chamber recreates the empire, complete with rivers and oceans filled with mercury. Those who helped construct the tomb likely were buried alive inside to keep them from sharing its secrets with the world.

Shi Huangdi's terracotta army remained buried until it was found by well-diggers in 1974.

SHIFTING POWER

The ruler was at the center of the Chinese government, but he did not work alone. During the Shang dynasty, the Chinese king ruled the area around the capital. Lands farther out were generally administered by other members of the royal family. Because positions in Shang society were based on a family relationship with the king, there was little opportunity for anyone else to reach the top ranks of society.

Family ties remained the basis of social class during the early Zhou period. In order to maintain control of lands far from the capital, the Zhou king distributed small outlying states to members of the royal family to administer as feudal lords. The lords established small, walled towns, where they served as rulers of the

Chinese rulers of every dynasty traveled with ceremony, especially when entering a conquered city.

lands and peoples assigned to them. The rulers of each state sent the king **tribute** and raised armies to fight for the king when needed.

The ruler of a feudal state appointed a handful of people called ministers who helped him govern. Often, the ruler's brothers or sons served as his ministers. They were rewarded for their loyalty and service with grants of land. Together, the state's ruler and ministers made up the aristocracy, or highest social class. The sons of ministers made up the next social class, known as the *shi*, or gentlemen. Shi often served as minor government officials or warriors.

Over time, the close ties between the Zhou king and the rulers of his states began to weaken and the feudal system began to lose importance. During the Warring States period, it fell apart altogether. As the most powerful states began to destroy or absorb other states, the aristocrats of the defeated states lost their position at the top of society. They were replaced by the shi, who were appointed as advisers and government administrators based on their education and skills. In addition to sons of former aristocrats, the shi class now also included some educated commoners.

By the time of the Qin dynasty, the gov-

ernment employed thousands of officials as part of a complex **bureaucracy**. In place of feudal states, the Qin divided the country into counties. Each county was ruled by an official appointed on the basis of military merit rather than birth. These officials remained subject to strong control by the central government.

A strong central government remained important during the Han dynasty. Under emperors such as Wudi, who ruled from 141 to 87 B.C., the Han sought educated men for government positions. The highest post was that of the imperial chancellor. Under him were a number of ministers who headed different governmental departments. Local officials were appointed by the central government to posts throughout China. Those who proved successful could be promoted, while those who failed in their duties would be demoted or dismissed.

As emperors appointed qualified men to serve in government positions, the importance of education grew, and schools began to emerge during the Warring States period. Boys began to attend school around age 10. After completing elementary school, they might receive an advanced education from a traveling teacher. These

Government officials such as county magistrates were tested on their knowledge and skills.

teachers generally presented their own ideas about a variety of subjects, spending time discussing and debating them with their students. Among the teachers active at this time was a man named Kong Fuzi, or Confucius. Confucius was a member of the shi class. He accepted young men from all social classes into his school, where he taught archery, charioteering, culture, music, **calligraphy**, and mathematics. In addition, Confucius examined the structure of government, society, and the family. He emphasized the importance of loyalty and filial piety (respect for parents and authorities).

Confucius's ideas were not immediately accepted, but as time went on, they became more popular. During the reign of the emperor Wudi, Confucianism became the official **ideology** of China, and in 124 B.C., Wudi founded a university for the study of Confucianism. There, students were expected to memorize 425,000 words from classic Confucian writings. After completing their university studies, young men took a series of exams. Those who passed could be considered for a governmental post.

While young men were out receiving their education, young women generally remained at home. Chinese women were considered inferior to men. They were not involved in politics and had no right to inherit land. A few upper-class women did receive an education, however. Some served as doctors to female patients in the emperor's household.

In general, Chinese parents of any social class had little interest in bearing daughters, since they would not be a permanent part of the family. Once a Chinese girl was married, she joined her husband's family. Most girls were married between the ages of 13 and 16. Like rulers, upper-class men might have several concubines, or "unofficial" wives.

Most upper-class families lived in large homes built around a central courtyard, some of which were several stories high. Walls and roof tiles were often painted bright colors, and openings for windows might be cut into the shape of an animal or other elaborate figures.

When the wealthy left their homes, they traveled in fine carriages covered with gold and silver decorations. Even their horses wore jeweled breastplates. The carriages of the wealthy often carried them to lavish banquets at the homes of other nobles. There people dressed in elegant silks leaned against cushions on the floor as they enjoyed exotic dishes. On the menu might be pheasant, quail, turtle, pork, dog, horse, or tiger meat. Each dish was prepared with a perfect blend of spices. As they ate, feasters were entertained by musicians, dancers, and jugglers.

Like the emperors, the upper class also prepared for the afterlife by building elaborate tombs. They were buried with statues, instruments, and other goods, though on a much smaller scale than the emperors. In early times, human sacrifices also accompanied the wealthy into the grave, but later, these were replaced by small statues.

Han farmers grew rice in paddy fields, still a typical method in China and other parts of Asia today.

GODS, ANCESTORS, AND BELIEFS

Ancient Chinese religion was not based on one set of ideas or teachings. Instead, it was constantly changing with the times. During the Shang dynasty, the people worshiped many gods. The supreme god was known as Di or Shangdi. Di was believed to control the weather, the harvest, and warfare. He also ruled over all other gods, such as the nature gods found in mountains, rivers, and forests.

Along with the gods, the ancient Chinese worshiped their ancestors. In order to keep the ancestors happy and comfortable in the afterlife, people made sacrifices to them. In return, the spirits of the ancestors would help the people by communicating with

Throughout history, the Chinese have followed various belief systems (such as Buddhism).

Di on behalf of the living. In general, only the ancestors of the king and other royal family members had an impact on the fate of the country. Thus, kings and other rulers often built ancestral halls to worship their ancestors. Scholars still question whether commoners worshiped their ancestors. They may have had **altars** in their home for this purpose.

The king was the most important religious leader in Shang society. Only he could make sacrifices to deceased kings. During the early part of the Shang dynasty, the kings were counted among the **shamans**. Shamans performed a number of rituals and were believed to be able to communicate with spirits, heal people, and control the weather. Shamans remained common, especially in rural areas, throughout much of ancient Chinese history. They were joined by a number of specialized priests who kept records, made predictions for the future, read dreams, or helped carry out rituals.

Among the most important rituals were sacrifices to the royal ancestors. At such sacrifices, the ancestors were offered grain, wine, animals, and human beings. More than 1,000 people were sometimes killed during a single sacrifice.

The Shang believed that the bodies of those who were sacrificed would offer nourishment to the ancestors. Some sacrifices were carried out on specific dates each year. Others were held when the Shang needed something—such as rain, military victory, or help after a natural disaster—from the ancestors. If their request was not granted after a sacrifice, the Shang blamed themselves for doing something wrong during the ceremony. In addition to sacrifices, the Shang also held elaborate banquets at which food and drink were offered to the ancestors in expensive bronze vessels.

While sacrifices and banquets were intended to please the ancestors, divination was used to learn their will. Whenever the king had a question about some matter of state—such as war, hunting, or the harvest—or about whether a sacrifice was acceptable, he turned to divination. The king's question was inscribed on an ox bone or tortoise shell. Then a priest touched the bone or shell with a hot metal poker to make cracks in it. The king and priest interpreted the cracks to learn the ancestors' answer. They often inscribed the answer on the bone or shell.

The establishment of the Zhou dynasty

About 200,000 oracle bone fragments have been found, dating to between 1400 and 1200 B.C.

THE DEVELOPMENT
OF ROAD AND CANAL
SYSTEMS THROUGHOUT
CHINA AND THE USE
OF COINS ENABLED
DEVELOPMENT OF
TRADE BETWEEN STATES.

brought with it a number of changes to the Chinese religion. A new supreme deity—Tian—was worshiped above Di. The Zhou king built temples to Tian and prayed to him for a good harvest. The kings also claimed to get their authority from Tian, who gave them a mandate to rule as Sons of Heaven. During the Shang period, many priests had held positions in the civil government along with their priestly duties. But now, government and priestly offices were usually separated. Additional priestly roles were established as well. Some priests oversaw elements of ritual dancing, while others performed prayers or practiced *astrology*. Priests continued to practice divination, but instead of interpreting cracks in ox bones and tortoise shells, they foretold the future by casting sticks to the ground and reading the pattern they made. A document called the *I Ching*, or *Book of Changes*, provided the diagrams used in interpretation.

Religion changed little during the Qin period, but during the later Han, traditional religious practice declined in importance. Although the gods and ancestors continued to be worshiped, many people turned to the new religions of Confucianism, Daoism, and Buddhism.

When Confucius began to share his *philosophy* in the late sixth century B.C., he had no intention of beginning a religion. After his death, however, Confucius's students expanded upon his ideas, and Confucius eventually came to be seen as divine, or godlike. Followers of Confucius believed that everyone had a role in society and that fulfilling that role was a *moral* duty. Since the family was at the center of society, a person's most important role was as a child who showed respect for his or her parents. In addition, people were supposed to do good, act unselfishly, and show concern for others. Acting in accordance with tradition was also emphasized.

Another religion, known as Daoism, developed around the same time as Confucianism. Daoists opposed the idea that people should follow traditions or the rules set out by Confucianism. Instead, they urged people to live a simple life, apart from the rest of society. Daoists tried to live in harmony with nature. They worshiped three deities, known as the Three Celestial Worthies (or Pure Ones), and sought ways to have everlasting life.

Despite the differences between Confucianism and Daoism, by the Han dynasty, many people were practicing both religions. A person might subscribe to Confucian ideas about service and authority while performing official government duties but then seek the quiet meditation of Daoism in his private life. During the late Han period, another new religion—Buddhism—was introduced. Buddhism had developed in India during the 500s B.C. and was carried to China by traders during the first century A.D. Buddhists came up with the belief in reincarnation, or being born in another body after death. They urged people to eliminate desire from their lives in order to achieve a state of spiritual joy known as nirvana.

The Qin may not have changed religion, but they did standardize coins, weights, and measures.

WAY OF THE WARRIOR

Although the land of China was largely isolated from potential enemies by natural barriers, the Chinese did face frequent invasions by nomadic tribes from the north. At various times in Chinese history, people in one state also faced the possibility of invasion by the people of a neighboring state. In order to defend their borders, the Chinese began building thick walls made of hard-packed earth, stone, or wood during the Zhou dynasty. At first, there were several separate walls, but the Qin connected and extended the various walls to make one 3,000-mile-long (4,828 km) wall on China's northern border. The Han built on to the wall as well, extending it westward into the Gobi Desert.

Mongol warriors, who were expert horsemen, threatened Chinese states from the north.

As China defended itself with barricades, the country's army also went on the offensive. Rulers frequently initiated wars to expand their territory as well as to seize **booty** and captives who could be used for sacrifices. Although the purposes for warfare remained relatively unchanged throughout China's history, the structure and makeup of its army changed drastically over time.

During the Shang dynasty, the army was made up of aristocrats who had pledged their loyalty to the king in return for grants of land. Aristocrats had both the money to purchase chariots and the time to train for fighting from them. Each chariot was pulled by two or four horses and carried three men: a driver, an archer, and a lancer. Infantry, or foot soldiers (recruited from among the commoners), likely accompanied the chariots, but they did not play a large role in battle. The total fighting force probably numbered around 3,000 to 5,000 men.

During the Shang and early Zhou dynasties, wars were ritualized affairs. They were usually held at specific times of the year to avoid bad weather and to avoid disrupting the agricultural work of soldiers who were also farm-

ers. When it was time for battle, the leaders of the opposing armies issued a challenge to one another. Then both sides attacked, using bronze-tipped spears and **halberds**, bows, and swords. During the fighting, soldiers observed a code of honor. Armies did not attack at night, and they did not send more chariots onto the battlefield than the number previously agreed upon. After the battle, the members of the losing army were often taken captive; some became human sacrifices.

Throughout the early Zhou and much of the Spring and Autumn period, the rulers of the various states raised their own armies. The ruler of each state also served as the head of its army. In addition, the Zhou king controlled a standing army with troops stationed throughout China. During wartime, the king's forces were joined by those of the states. Although chariots were still widely used, by the end of the Spring and Autumn period, armies were coming to rely more on infantry conscripted from among the peasants. In areas with challenging terrain, soldiers on foot could fight where chariots could not. The additional infantry made armies larger, with total forces of 10,000 men or more in some states.

Conscription was eventually abandoned in favor of soldiers who would serve for longer terms.

Did You Know?

———

AMONG THE MOST
FAMOUS MILITARY
STRATEGISTS DURING
THE SPRING AND
AUTUMN PERIOD WAS
SUNZI, OR SUN TZU,
WHOSE BOOK *THE ART OF
WAR* IS STILL READ TODAY.

———

During battle, the two sides lined up on opposite ends of the battlefield before coming together for the fight. Charioteers used bows, while the infantry wielded lances. Zhou-period battles generally lasted two days or less, and a campaign was usually over within a few months. As during the Shang period, a code of honor governed a soldier's behavior. Zhou armies did not attack before their enemy had had time to line up, and even during a chariot chase, the warriors on opposite sides were expected to speak courteously to one another. Even so, at the end of a battle, the losing soldiers might be taken as slaves or sacrificial victims.

The Warring States period brought about a drastic change in warfare. Codes of honor were eliminated completely. Chariots were largely replaced by infantry in most states, and the aristocracy became less important in the army. Instead, soldiers were led by experienced generals. Fighting forces grew enormous, reaching into the hundreds of thousands in many states. At the same time, some states introduced a cavalry (horse-riding unit) into their armies consisting of only 5,000 or so soldiers.

Armies also began to emphasize strategy during the Warring States period and attempted to outsmart their opponents. They might light campfires in an attempt to lure an enemy to the wrong position. Spies also sought out information on an enemy's plans. Siege warfare became popular. A siege could last more than a year. On the field, fighting became more intense, with a single battle lasting up to 10 days.

Constant warfare brought about major advances in weapons technology, including the introduction of the crossbow. This new weapon could fire its short, heavy arrows up to 650 feet (198 m) to pierce a shield or thick leather armor. As a result of such weapons, Warring States battles were more deadly. A single battle could result in nearly half a million casualties on the losing side. Victors often cut off the ears of dead enemies to keep track of their kills.

Warfare during the Qin and Han dynasties remained similar to that of the Warring States period, with an emphasis on infantry over chariots. Members of the cavalry may have been volunteers from among wealthy families. The infantry, on the other hand, was conscripted from among the common people. All non-noble men between the ages of 25 and 60 were required to serve in the army. They first completed two years of service, after which they could return home until they were called up during wartime. Newly conscripted soldiers often served at posts along the defensive walls on China's borders. They lived in watchtowers built along the wall and served as border guards.

Successful soldiers could be promoted into the officer ranks of the army. If they were successful as officers, they might be rewarded with land or slaves. Such rewards led some men to become professional soldiers.

Authorship of *The Art of War* is disputed, since the text may postdate Sun Tzu's lifetime.

AMONG THE MILLIONS

The majority of China's population—which totaled 60 million by the first century B.C.—was made up of peasants, or farmers. During the early part of the Zhou dynasty, peasants generally worked the lands of feudal lords. In return for their service, the peasants received food and clothing for their families.

As the feudal system broke down during the Warring States period, some peasants were able to buy their own land. Life was hard for independent farmers, though. In order to pay the high taxes required by their state, they might have to borrow money. If they couldn't repay it, they would have to sell the land, which was quickly scooped up by the wealthy. Peasants were again forced to work land that was not

Iron plows, invented during the Han dynasty, originally required two oxen or buffalo to pull.

their own, this time as **tenant** farmers who had to pay expensive rents to landlords. This process continued and even became more common during the Han dynasty.

Like farmers, artisans worked for their living. They produced everyday items such as ceramic utensils as well as intricate bronze vessels and delicate jade carvings to be used in the tombs of the wealthy. During the early parts of China's history, many feudal manors were self-sufficient and produced their own necessities. As the feudal system declined, independent workshops grew in importance. By the Han period, there were numerous private workshops in addition to government-run factories that produced iron and bronze weapons and tools.

As artisans began to create more products, a class of traders sprung up. Cities and towns opened markets filled with shops and stalls. People from all classes of society strolled among the shops. In one area, they would find fruits and vegetables. In another, live animals. Other sections of the market sold clothing, tools, or pots and pans. As they wandered through the market, shoppers were entertained by jugglers, acrobats, and fortune-tellers.

Beginning in the Han dynasty, many merchants participated in international trade via the Silk Road. This "road" was actually a system of trails that led 4,000 miles (6,437 km) from China to the Mediterranean Sea. The trails wound through steep mountains and stark deserts, but the reward for those willing to brave the journey was great. Chinese goods such as silk, jade, perfumes, and spices were in demand in the **West**, and they brought high prices. In addition, traders carried goods such as gold, jewels, and glass from the West to be sold in China.

Local and international trade made many merchants rich. Yet, because they did not have to labor for their money, merchants were looked down upon by other members of society. Although artisans did not become as rich as merchants, they were generally looked upon more favorably because they produced objects for the good of society. Since farmers provided the most essential product—food—they were regarded more highly still. Even so, farmers were among the poorest people in China. Many farmers eventually abandoned their land for an easier life in the city as an artisan or merchant.

The traditional silk-making process begins with unwinding strands from silkworm cocoons.

Did You Know?

BY THE END OF THE

HAN DYNASTY, THE

UNIVERSITY ESTABLISHED

BY EMPEROR WUDI

ATTRACTED MORE THAN

30,000 STUDENTS.

No matter what their job, commoners were required to serve as conscripted laborers. During the Han dynasty, men between the ages of 15 and 56 served 1 month a year in the labor force. Laborers built temples, palaces, and tombs; constructed roads and canals; and worked in government industries. Among the largest projects completed by conscripted laborers was the Great Wall built during the Qin dynasty, which may have involved the labor of 300,000 men over a period of 10 years. Thousands died while working on it.

While men worked at their jobs and served in the labor corps, women had their own work to do. Peasant women helped with farm chores, and many raised silkworms, a kind of caterpillar. They collected the silkworm cocoons, and then spun the silk from them into thread. A few women also set up shop as artisans, and the widow of a merchant might take over his business. Women were also in charge of preparing their family's food, which included cakes of grain, vegetables, and, occasionally, meat.

During China's early history, the children of commoners generally learned the same jobs as their parents. Later, however, as teachers such as Confucius began to travel the country, even common people sought an education. Learning made it possible to improve one's social position, as the government began to recruit the most qualified people for official positions, regardless of birth.

Although commoners could better their position in society, slaves could not. Scholars disagree, however, over the extent of slavery in ancient China. Some find no evidence that slavery was practiced during the Shang or Zhou dynasties. Others believe that non-Chinese prisoners of war may have been forced to tend livestock or farmland. By the Han period, slaves made up only about 5 percent of the population. In general, slaves came from among prisoners of war, criminals, or children sold into slavery to pay off debts. The children of slaves automatically became slaves. Most slaves remained in service for life, but a few were freed, especially when they became too old to be useful to their masters.

Many slaves likely worked in the homes of the elite. Most commoners, however, lived far from the wealthy. Peasants generally lived in the countryside, in one-room huts with dirt floors. Even in the city, the wealthy lived in one section, while the common people crowded into another area at the city's edge. The homes of the poorest were small and bare, dug partly into the ground and covered with a thatched roof. Wealthier artisans and merchants constructed three-room homes, with the middle room built higher than those on the sides.

The graves of commoners also differed drastically from those of the wealthy. In place of the elaborate tombs of the aristocracy, commoners generally had no tomb. They might not even have a coffin, although the deceased was sometimes left with one or two coins to help him make his way in the afterlife.

Commoners would not have had access to books, which were sometimes encased in cloth or wood.

LEGACY OF AN EMPIRE

Ancient Chinese society experienced a series of changes throughout its history. Those changes continued during the last years of the Han dynasty as more and more peasants were forced to sell out to wealthy landowners. Natural disasters left the farmers even poorer, and soon riots and rebellions broke out across the country. In the upper reaches of society, there was also trouble. A series of child-emperors were crowned between A.D. 88 and 220. Since they were not old enough to rule on their own, they were assisted by their mothers—the empress dowagers—as well as palace officials known as eunuchs. A power struggle quickly broke out between the empress dowagers and the eunuchs, and the eunuchs eventually

By the final dynasty, the Qing, courtly dress for queens and empress dowagers was most ornate.

emerged successful. They were not strong enough to put down the rebellions that continued to break out across the country, however, and in 220, they were overthrown. The Han dynasty—and ancient Chinese history—was at an end.

For the next 350 years, China was split—first into 3 kingdoms and then into 16. The kingdoms were almost continuously at war. Finally, in 581, the Chinese empire was reunited under the Sui dynasty. The Sui were followed by the Tang, Song, Mongol, Ming, and Qing dynasties, in an empire that was finally overthrown by revolutionaries in 1912.

Although the Chinese empire came to an end, China still exists today, and much of modern Chinese culture can be traced back to its earliest history. The Chinese continue to honor their ancestors, for example, and many people still practice Buddhism. Confucian and Dao-

ist thought also influence Chinese society and education today. The writing system used in China is based on that developed during the Shang dynasty. And even the idea of China itself comes from ancient times. Despite being spread across a huge land and encompassing different *ethnic* groups, the Chinese still see themselves as a united people living in the Middle Kingdom.

Today, millions of tourists flock to sites such as the tomb of Shi Huangdi or sections of the Great Wall. And archaeologists continue to discover new information about China's past. That information reveals a complex society made up of millions of people. In the earliest times, those people were stuck in their social classes. Later, there were greater opportunities to improve their social standing. But no matter where a person fit into society, each individual contributed to the rich culture now known as ancient China.

Merchant caravans traveled from the Mediterranean to China for goods such as silk.

c. 2070 B.C. — The Xia dynasty begins, and China is first united under a king.

c. 1600 B.C. — The Shang dynasty comes to power.

c. 1046 B.C. — The Zhou dynasty overthrows the Shang, claiming to have a Mandate from Heaven to rule.

c. 770 B.C. — The Spring and Autumn period begins as the Zhou king loses power to the rulers of China's states.

551 B.C. — The teacher Confucius is born.

c. 500 B.C. — Iron is used to make tools and weapons.

c. 476 B.C. — Rulers of the states fight for power as the Warring States period begins.

c. 400 B.C. — Coins are introduced as currency.

221 B.C. — The state of Qin unites China and sets up the Chinese empire under the first emperor, Shi Huangdi.

215 B.C. — Construction on the Qin Great Wall begins.

213 B.C. — Shi Huangdi orders the burning of books.

210 B.C. — Shi Huangdi dies.

206 B.C. — The Qin dynasty is overthrown and the first Han emperor, Liu Bang, takes the throne.

165 B.C. — An exam system is established for men seeking a government position.

141 B.C. — Emperor Wudi takes the throne.

124 B.C. — Wudi establishes a university for Confucian teaching.

c. A.D. 65 — Buddhism is introduced to China from India.

A.D. 88 — The first of several child-emperors succeeds to the throne.

A.D. 105 — Historical records first indicate the use of paper.

A.D. 220 — The Han dynasty falls.

ALTARS: special tables used for carrying out religious rituals

ASTROLOGY: the study of the stars and planets in the belief that they influence events and people on Earth

BUREAUCRACY: a group of government workers

BOOTY: money or goods taken from a defeated enemy in war

CALLIGRAPHY: the art of making decorative handwriting

CONSCRIPTED: required to serve in the military or a labor force

DYNASTIES: series of rulers from the same family line

ETHNIC: relating to a group of people with a shared racial, cultural, religious, or national background

FEUDAL: having to do with the system of feudalism, in which peasants farm the land of a lord in return for food and protection; the lord provides money or military service to a king or other ruler

HALBERDS: weapons made of a long-handled spear with an ax head mounted to the end

IDEOLOGY: a set of ideas held by a group or culture or on which a government or political system is based

IMPERIAL: having to do with an empire

JADE: a hard, green gemstone

MORAL: relating to right and wrong behaviors

NOMADIC: moving from place to place, rather than settling in one location

PHILOSOPHY: the study of ethics, logic, and other ideas

SHAMANS: in some religions, a priest or priestess who is believed to be able to communicate with spirits, heal illnesses, and control nature

TENANT: someone who rents a home or land from the property owner

TRIBUTE: a payment made by a weaker nation to a stronger one, often because of conquest or for protection

WEST: the part of the world that includes Europe and the Americas

Selected Bibliography

Blunden, Caroline, and Mark Elvin. *Cultural Atlas of China*. New York: Checkmark Books, 1998.

Ebrey, Patricia Buckley. *Cambridge Illustrated History of China*. New York: Cambridge University Press, 1996.

Enzheng, Tong. "Magicians, Magic, and Shamanism in Ancient China." *Journal of East Asian Archaeology* 4, no. 1 (2002): 27–73. doi: http://dx.doi.org /10.1163/156852302322454495.

Hsu, Cho-Yun. *Ancient China in Transition: An Analysis of Social Mobility, 722–222 B.C.* Stanford, Calif.: Stanford University Press, 1965.

Kleeman, Terry, and Tracy Barrett. *The Ancient Chinese World*. New York: Oxford University Press, 2005.

Loewe, Michael, and Edward L. Shaughnessy, eds. *The Cambridge History of Ancient China: From the Origins of Civilization to 221 B.C.* New York: Cambridge University Press, 1999.

Murowchick, Robert E., ed. *China: Ancient Culture, Modern Land*. Norman: University of Oklahoma Press, 1994.

Scarpari, Maurizio. *Ancient China: Chinese Civilization from Its Origins to the Tang Dynasty*. New York: Barnes & Noble, 2006.

Websites

THE BRITISH MUSEUM: ANCIENT CHINA

http://www.ancientchina.co.uk/menu.html

Explore ancient Chinese objects, workshops, and tombs.

A VISUAL SOURCEBOOK OF CHINESE CIVILIZATION

http://depts.washington.edu/chinaciv/

Find information, pictures, and timelines about ancient Chinese civilization.

Note: Every effort has been made to ensure that the websites listed above are suitable for children, that they have educational value, and that they contain no inappropriate material. However, because of the nature of the Internet, it is impossible to guarantee that these sites will remain active indefinitely or that their contents will not be altered.